Hacking for Beginners: Your Guide for Learning the Basics of Hacking and Kali Linux

various sources. Please consult a licensed professional before attempting any techniques outlined in this book.

By reading this document, the reader agrees that under no circumstances are is the author responsible for any losses, direct or indirect, which are incurred as a result of the use of information contained within this document, including, but not limited to, —errors, omissions, or inaccuracies.

Table of Content

3) Hping3

Why do we want to scan the network ?

IV. Malware and Cyber Attacks

1) What is a Malware ?

1) Viruses

2) Trojans

3) Worms

4) Ransomware

5) Adware

6) Spyware

2) Examples of Cyber Attacks

What is a Cyber Attack?

What is a MITM (Man In The Middle) attack ?

1) MAC Spoofing

2) ARP Spoofing

> # sudo **ettercap –i eth0 –T -w /root/scan.txt –M arp /192.168.1.3 /**

3) Rogue DHCP Server

    a.   # echo "1" > /proc/sys/net/ipv4/ip_forward

    a.   # sudo **apt-get install isc-dhcp-server**

    a.   # nano /etc/dhcp/dhcpd.conf

    a.   # sudo **ip route add default via** 192.168.1.1

How can we protect ourselves from a MITM attack?

What is a DoS (Denial of Service) attack?

What is a DDoS (Distributed Denial of Service) attack?

    1) Brute Force

    2) Dictionary attack

    3) Rainbow table

Or <u>Click Here to Download</u> <u>(https://ramonnastase.com/kindle-security/)</u>

Also, I kindly ask you to **leave a review** after finishing this book. It will help me a lot. Thank you and happy reading ! ☺

Introduction

First of all I want to congratulate you and thank you for taking the decision to **invest in yourself and to become better.** I want to tell you this guide will take from 0 (in the field of Cyber Security) and will lead you to a basic level so that you are aware of the things that happen around us on the Internet every day.

I want this book to change you. To change your mentality, the way you think and give you a new perspective on things. The concepts explained here are both theoretical and practical.

Let me show you a few of the stuff that you are going to learn from this book

- How **Hackers** think
- What are the **5 steps** of **Hacking**
- How to **scan devices** in a network
- How to see other people's **traffic** (such as passwords and web sessions)
- How to use **Kali Linux**

This book is structured in 3 chapters that cover different themes, belonging to the basic concepts of CyberSecurity. One thing I want you to know is that if you are starting for the first time in IT, this book is not the right choice. Why ? Because you need Linux (at least average) knowledge, networking and (little) programming to understand some of the things that I explain here.

That's why I want to tell you (from the very beginning) that: before you learn to break and secure things, it's important to understand how technology works. Having this in mind, I wish you a lot of strength in what you do, pull as hard as you can, in the end, you will see, with constant work and effort you will achieve what you have done.

Best regards,
Ramon Nastase

PS: in case you have questions you can contact me via email, or on my website. (https://ramonnastase.com)

I. The Hacking Process

Generally, when talking about Hacking, there is a very well-thought-out structure in the back. We do not want to find a server and "jump" directly on it because we have too little information about it at the moment and we are at risk of being caught if we do not take into account the 5 steps in the process.

How does the Hacking process work?

I hope you notice that I have said "the Hacking process," which can take a few days, weeks, even months (depending on the target and the risk). This process, as I said earlier, consists of 5 steps (Figure 1.1):

1. **Reconnaissance** - Information Gathering
2. **Scanning**
3. **Gaining Access**
4. **Maintaining Access**
5. **Covering Tracks**

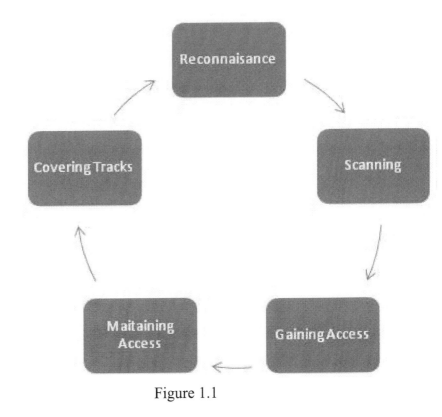

Figure 1.1

And now let's take one turn and talk about each one:

1) Reconnaissance - *"Information Gathering"*

One of the most important things that Hackers do when they decide to attack a system (server, network, etc.) is to gather as much data as possible about it.

Think in the following way: when you want to go for a holiday in a place / country where you have not been, what are you doing? Most likely, you do homework. You mean you're interested in that location. You are looking for different things on Google (what you can do there, such as weather / food, reviews of places in the area, etc.). In other words, you **inform yourself about your target**.

Exactly through this process a hacker passes when he decides to attack a system. There are different ways you can learn more about a site / server, one of the simplest methods is to search Google for information about it.

With a simple command like **nslookup** (or **dig**), you can find out with the IP address of a site, and with the whois command you can find out more about that domain.

```
> nslookup google.com
> whois google.com
```

The term Reconnaissance (or Information Gathering) comes from the idea of researching, informing you about a particular topic before moving on to action. In short, basically it means **documenting** before the **action**.

As a matter of time this process is most "expensive". Why? Because an attacker needs to be very well informed, he needs to know things in detail because otherwise (as we said in step # 5) risk his own freedom.

2) Scanning (the system)

The next step in the "Hacking Process" is **scanning**. Once a Hacker has more information about his target, he will begin to learn more (technically this time). And how will he do that? Using a variety of tools (such as Nmap) to scan networks, servers, and provide clearer information about network topology, used equipment, operating system, and more.

Why are they important? Why is it important for a Hacker to know if a particular web server is running on Windows or Linux? Because once it has this information it can go further (step 3) with a little research on Google to discover some existing vulnerabilities and try to take advantage of them in order to gain access to that system (or to extract certain data).

About scanning and the various ways we can do this, we'll talk more broadly in Chapter 6. Using these scanned data, the Hacker will move to step # 3.

3) Gaining Access

Having done the themes (done research, scanned networks / servers, learned information from different sources - Google, Facebook, Forums - about the target), the hacker can start the attack. The attack should be very well thought to be in stealth mode (without triggering alarms and - if possible - without generating too many logs).

There are a lot of **tools** (*Burp Suite, SQLmap, Metasploit,* etc.) that can be used to generate a cyber attack, everything depends on technology and objective.

Getting access can be done in several ways and from several points of view:
- Getting **root** access on a Linux server
- Obtain access to a **site's** administration **panel**

- Obtaining **access** to a particular **network** equipment (Router, Firewall, Switch etc.)
- Get **access** to a network's **end device** (smart phone, tablet, laptop, etc.)

Once the hacker has access to one of the items listed earlier, he is infiltrated into the network and can get a lot of information about the organization he is (digital).

We will discuss in Chapter 5 more about some types of cyber attacks and how we can do them.

4) Maintaining Access

Once in the network, Hacker has the option of retaining access. In many situations when different servers of major companies (Yahoo, Google, Microsoft, etc.) have been broken, Hackers have always left open doors to get back into the system.

These wickets are called **"backdoor"** and are intentionally left by Hackers (or even by the software developers of any applications that you and I use day by day) to have access later in the system.

So they can constantly extract data, track what's happening in organizations, hold back control, and then do something with these data (usually they are sold on the black market on the Deep Web).

After this process, step # 5 is very important.

5) Covering Tracks

This is a very important process (the "Trace Coverage" feature). A process that many Hackers (especially those who are at the beginning of the road) omit it. They are simply not mindful (or aware) of covering their tracks and getting caught (in the US, by the FBI, CIA or the NSA) and punished in court for their deeds.

I repeat that **unauthorized access** to a system can lead to serious criminal consequences:
- confiscation of computer goods - laptops, external hard drives, etc.
- placing under supervision
- or even arrest, these being just some of the consequences

In order not to leave such traces with the possibility to be discovered, here comes a key element: *TO UNDERSTAND HOW THE TECHNOLOGY WORKS*

What am I talking about? I refer to the fact that it is extremely important to understand how "that database server, that mail or web server" works - both in terms of how you configure it and in terms of monitoring and logging it.

It's also important to know how to run the **Windows** or **Linux** operating system. "How are users created? Where are their data stored? Login data? What happens when you log on to such a system? Where are those logs written? "

Hacking (professional, ethical and safe) is *not for everyone*, and that's why you have to be very well prepared because some situations your freedom can be put into play.

Another very important thing I want you to remember is that no one, **NO ONE**, does "Hacking" from their **home**. It's very important to hide your tracks as much as you can. This is to change your location, use VPN services and / or Tor for encryption and traffic anonymity.

How do we delete tracks in a system?

Now let's take a look at some of the ways you can cover your footprints once you have entered a system (network, server, laptop, etc.)

- **Delete logs from different applications (web, mail, etc.)**
- **Delete User Logs**
- **Delete logs from different monitoring systems**

Each system has different ways to monitor it for debugging or troubleshooting in the event of a problem

To do this, it is not necessary, like a hacker, to go step by step from file to file to look for and delete the latest logs. But it can use different existing scriptures (on the Internet) of other people with whom they can clean up their traces.

Here's an example of a **Windows** program (also you can use the Event Viewer from any Windows machine) that does the job for you :)

On **Linux** you can use the following commands:

#rm ./bash_history - to delete the commands given by the current user

#vim /var/log/messages - a place where you can delete the logs that have been generated

Or in any other file in **/var/log**, depends on which application was attempting to exploit. There is another way we can delete the logs using Meterpreter (an application for PenTers.

6) (For the ethical) Reporting

Another very important step, especially in the Ethical Hacking process, is # 6, Reporting, the step in which Hacker generates a report on the vulnerabilities found (and exploited), the ways in which they can be corrected, and other information that will lead to solve and secure the system.

These were the 5 steps (6 for Ethical Hackers) that **make the Hacking process**. In the next chapter, we will start discussing the three fundamental elements underlying cyber security.

II. Installing and using the Hacker's OS Kali Linux

If you're curious to find out how to do cyber attacks, then you've come to the right chapter because now I'm going to show you a tutorial to install Kali Linux (the Linux distribution used by Hackers).

What is Kali Linux?

Kali Linux is the **Linux distribution** (most) used by Hackers and Professional Pen Testers due to the number of programs pre-installed on it. In Kali Linux you can find a lot of programs focused on security and on the vulnerability testing side. Whether we're talking about scans, DoS attacks, Web attacks or any other kind of attack, Kali is the perfect choice for whatever it takes to learn security. In Figure 2.1 below you can see the official logo of this Linux distribution. The name **Kali** comes from the god of war in Hindu mythology.

Figure 2.1

Although at first it may seem a little difficult to use, it does not have to discourage you from persevering and constantly learning new things. Why do I say it's hard to use? Well, first of all, it's Linux, and if you have not interacted with Linux so far (from the Terminal) it might seem quite difficult at first.

Second is the large number of Pen Testing programs on Kali. These are difficult to use (especially at the beginning) if you do not know what their purpose is (basically the technology behind that tool) and if you do not know its syntax (but this can be taught - just like the others).

How can we install Kali Linux ?

When it comes to installing any distributions of Linux (so Kali) we have 2 options:

- **Dual-Boot installation**
    - Linux and Windows are installed on different partitions
    - The 2 OSs run one at a time
    - Requires the laptop / desktop reboot to choose the desired OS
- **Virtual Machine Installation**
    - Linux comes installed in a Virtual Box and can be used in conjunction with Windows
    - It does not require reboot, and the two OSs can be used simultaneously
    - Consume more resources (CPU & RAM) because they must be allocated to 2 OSs at the same time

I personally prefer the 2nd method because it is much simpler and faster. In addition, I tell you from your own experience that if you use the first option you will often fail to enter into Linux and you will say, "Let another time. Now I do not want to restart. " But with the 2nd version you do not really apologize: D

To install Kali Linux, we need to go through a few steps. First of all, we need the **VirtualBox** program (or another virtualization program - ex: VMware Workstation) and the image of the Kali Linux OS (https://www.kali.org/downloads/) as you can see in Figure 3.2.

I recommend that you select the **64-bit version** and download it using Torrent for it will be much faster.

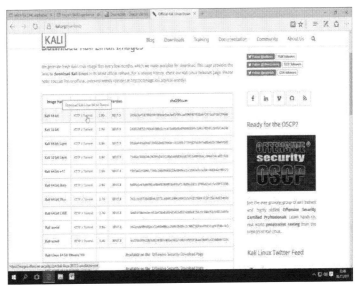

Figure 2.2

The next steps, after downloading the Kali Linux OS image and the Virtualbox virtualization program, are:

1. Start creating a virtual machine in VirtualBox

2. Starting the installation process - as you can see in figures 3.3 and 3.4.

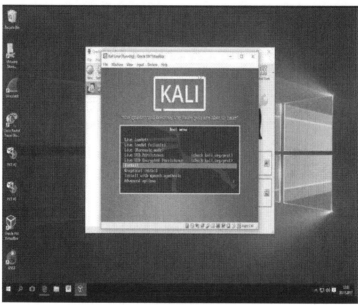

Figure 2.3

If you want to test Kali without installing it, then you can choose the **Live** option. The only problem is that every time you start the virtual machine you will delete the settings / work that you have submitted up to that point. If you write a script and you are in Live mode, it will be deleted, will not be saved!

So here I recommend going to the classic installation so that all your data is saved on disk.

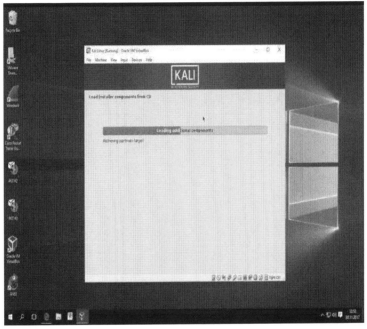

Figure 2.4

Following the installation process (Figure 2.4), you have to go **next -> next -> finish**, and then wait a while until everything is ready. If you do not manage at any given time (some settings that you do not understand or you are experiencing an error), I encourage you to make a great **research on Google**.

In the past few years, we have found that a skill, an increasingly **necessary skill** today is **searching on Google**. Probably amusing you what I'm saying here, but

I want you to know I'm serious about it. I am telling you from my own experience that this skill has made me very often out of the tangle, regardless of the situation I was in (building the site, finishing the projects during the faculty, documenting and last but not least finding the forums with topics of interest for me).

So if you get an installation error or any other situation. *Do not panic. Think for yourself. And search on Google :)*

Um .... and by the way, the **default** *user* for Kali Linux is **root** with the **toor** *password.* Now I've missed you a search;)

Working with Kali Linux

Now that you've finished installing and you've managed to get started and go to Desktop, I propose to move on and briefly introduce Kali so you can understand and identify some of the tools you have at mood (depending on your objective). As you can see in Figure 2.5, we are in Kali's default state, specifically on the Desktop. On the left you have a bar with some of the tools, but above all (on the 2nd position) you can see the terminal (most probably the most important component that I recommend you to master the best;).

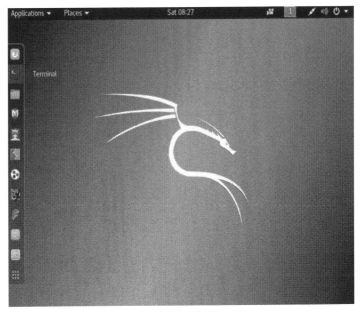

Figure 2.5

Going to the top left, we have a **very interesting menu** :D The Pen Testing application menu that we can use (some of you have just experienced the previous chapters). As you can see in Figure 2.6, we have a choice (or even more, they are in different categories, and here we intervene - to choose the most effective programs for our interest).

These applications are actually "hacking" programs that can be used with both good and less good intentions. It all depends on you now to use them for best (ps ... Ethical Hacking).

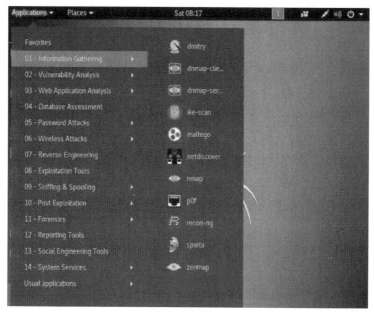

Figure 2.6

And as you can see, the very first category is called "Information Gathering", just like the **first step** in the **Hacking Process** (which we discussed in much more detail in Chapter 2). These tools you see in Figure 2.6 help us get more information about our target. Some of them have even used or mentioned them (nmap, zenmap).

One thing I want you to remember is that, when you hit one of these programs (whatever they may be), these two things can happen:
1. The program opens with the GUI interface
2. A terminal is running the program opens and displays its "help" information

In the first case it can be intuitive what you can do with it, you will realize it during use (examples of **GUI programs in Kali**: *Yersinia, Maltego, Burp suite, Wireshark* etc.).

In the 2nd case, it may not be so obvious from the first use, as, as I said before, you will open a terminal with a sort of help / description menu for that tool. In both cases (especially in case 2), it's important to learn that program. Understand what they really do and what to eat. In Figure 2.7 below, you can see exactly what I mean:

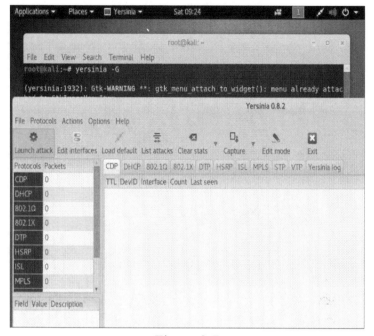

Figure 2.7

Yersinia is a graphical tool with which we can easily make MITM attacks (especially if there are Cisco - Routers, Unsecured Switches). Yersinia also has a variant in the terminal that is more powerful and customizable. To start the Yersinia GUI version I have to give the following command:

```
#yersinia -G
```

From here, I let you experiment with this program: D All I can tell you is that on the left side there will be the number of packets captured by that type (the statistics that give you a clear indication of what type of attack focus).

Going forward, in Figure 2.8 below, you can see another category that contains various tools (some of them used - *ettercap, Wireshark, macchanger*) that aim to listen to or capture traffic in an attack **MITM** (Man-In-The Middle) type:

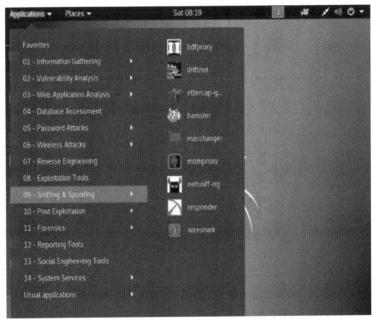

Figure 2.8

This was just a brief introduction of Kali Linux. In the following chapters we'll take a much more in depth look at some of the tools from this powerful Linux distribution.

III. Scanning the Servers and the Network

I'm sure you've heard of the concept of scanning a network (or the devices within the network). Well, in this chapter we'll talk in more detail about this subject and later on we'll see how to **scan networks and servers** (from just a few commands on Kali Linux or a few clicks on Windows).

What does "Scanning a Network" mean ?

Before we go over to see how I can scan a network, I want to explain what this scanning means. What do I mean by the end when I say I scanned the X.Y.Z.A network? I refer to the fact that I used a certain program (in this case **Nmap**) to find out which devices are connected to the network at the moment.

Not only did we find out what these devices are (see their **IP** address and **MAC** address) but we can find out more information like:

- The type of the device
- The OS and its version

- Open ports
- Network applications that run on those ports
- etc.

Once we have this information, we can use them to better understand how the network is structured, to scan and then test the network and vulnerability servers (in an ethical way) to make sure all devices are up & running. These, of course, are just a few reasons why scanning the network and the devices in it makes sense.

How do I scan a network?

Scanning the network (and its components) is easy, using Nmap. Nmap comes from Network Mapper and helps us "map" the network into an output (from the terminal) quite easy to understand. The program I use in the example below (for scanning the network) is called Nmap. **Nmap** (on Windows, the graphical interface program is called **Zenmap**) is a free tool extremely used by hackers and ethical hackers.

With its help we can discover the devices connected to the network, the open ports on them and even their Operating System.

Here are some examples of commands that we can give with Nmap to achieve different goals:

1) Scanning a network with Nmap

`# nmap -sP 192.168.1.0/24` -- ICMP (ping) scanning, displaying the number of

network devices (aka

PING **SCAN**)

`# nmap -sS 192.168.1.0/24` -- scanning the entire network to find ports

open (TCP, using

SYN) on each device

(aka **PORT SCAN**)

In Figure 3.1 below, you can see in detail the information about part of the equipment connected to the network (more precisely the Router with IP 192.168.1.1 and another device with the IP 192.168.1.3). Besides discovering that these devices are connected to the network, Nmap has also discovered open ports on these devices.

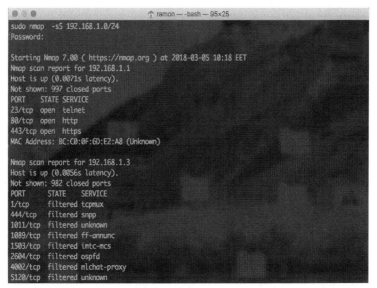

```
● ● ●                    ↑ ramon — -bash — 95×25
sudo nmap  -sS 192.168.1.0/24
Password:

Starting Nmap 7.00 ( https://nmap.org ) at 2018-03-05 10:18 EET
Nmap scan report for 192.168.1.1
Host is up (0.0071s latency).
Not shown: 997 closed ports
PORT    STATE SERVICE
23/tcp  open  telnet
80/tcp  open  http
443/tcp open  https
MAC Address: 8C:C0:0F:6D:E2:A8 (Unknown)

Nmap scan report for 192.168.1.3
Host is up (0.0056s latency).
Not shown: 982 closed ports
PORT     STATE    SERVICE
1/tcp    filtered tcpmux
444/tcp  filtered snpp
1011/tcp filtered unknown
1089/tcp filtered ff-annunc
1503/tcp filtered imtc-mcs
2604/tcp filtered ospfd
4002/tcp filtered mlchat-proxy
5120/tcp filtered unknown
```

Figure 3.1

As you can see, Router (192.168.1.1) has opened 3 important services that can be vulnerable and exploited. For example, port 23 represents Telnet, which means we can connect remotely to it, and we can even have access to the CLI.

Also, ports 80 and 443 that identify Web traffic is open (so we can connect through the browser and we can try to get access to this Router). Now I hope you understand the role and power of scanning;)

2) Scanning devices in a network with Nmap

#nmap -A *192.168.1.1* -- scans a single device for service delivery   (ports) and operating system (aka **OS SCAN**)

#nmap –sT 192.168.1.254 -- scans by using TCP packets

#nmap -sU 192.168.1.1 -- scans by using UDP packets

In Figure 3.2, you can see the result of the first command we also added and **-sS** for TCP port scanning:

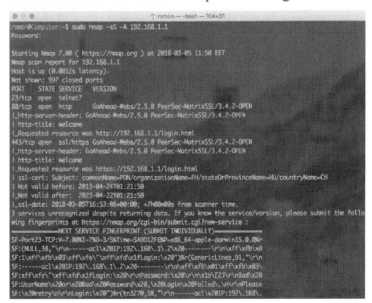

Figure 3.2

If you want to get (more) real-time scan-related information then I recommend you add **-v** to any kind of Nmap command you want.

You can also press "*Space*" to get data on scan progress (you will see X% completed and estimated time). Other examples of scanning using Nmap:

`#nmap -F 192.168.1.0/24`   -- scans every device in the network for the top 100

more used ports

`#nmap -sS -p 80,443,23,22,25 192.168.1.1` -- scans the device for the ports given with -p using TCP SYN packets

`#nmap -F -oN results.txt 192.168.1.0/24`   -- scans the network quickly and stores the result in the results.txt file (very useful for a Python script)

3) Hping3

Another very useful tool we can use next to Nmap is hping3. **Hping3** is a traffic generator, similar to ping, but with much more functionality. It is able to send (besides ICMP - ping traffic) packets of the TCP, UDP or RAW - IP type customized packages (with any specification we tell them about these protocols).

For example, we can send a TCP ACK packet,or FIN to see how the server or firewall that we want to test reacts. Below is a list of things you can do with this tool.

Practically, hping3 helps us do the following:
- Firewall testing
- Advanced port scanning
- Network testing, using different protocols, TOS, fragmentation
- Manual path MTU discovery
- Advanced traceroute, under all the supported protocols
- Remote OS fingerprinting
- Remote uptime guessing
- TCP/IP stacks auditing

Here are a few examples of **using hping3**:

`#hping3 -h`   -- to learn more about the available arguments

`#hping3 -1 VICTIM_IP`   -- a normal ping (ICMP) is sent (Figure 3.3)

`#hping3 --traceroute -V -1 | VICTIM_IP` -- a single traceroute package is sent to see where it is going

`#hping3 -V -S -p 80 VICTIM_IP` -- TCP SYN packets are sent on port 80

to see if the application responds

In Figure 3.3 below, we can do some tests and you can see some of the examples outlined above:

```
root@rn-s-1vcpu-1gb-fra1-01:~# hping3 -1 hackthissite.org
HPING hackthissite.org (eth0 198.148.81.137): icmp mode set, 28 headers + 0 data bytes
len=42 ip=198.148.81.137 ttl=51 id=9426 icmp_seq=0 rtt=169.2 ms
len=42 ip=198.148.81.137 ttl=51 id=10767 icmp_seq=1 rtt=169.0 ms
len=42 ip=198.148.81.137 ttl=51 id=12684 icmp_seq=2 rtt=168.9 ms
^C
--- hackthissite.org hping statistic ---
3 packets transmitted, 3 packets received, 0% packet loss
round-trip min/avg/max = 168.9/169.0/169.2 ms
root@rn-s-1vcpu-1gb-fra1-01:~# hping3 -V -S -p 80 hackthissite.org
using eth0, addr: 46.101.143.160, MTU: 1500
HPING hackthissite.org (eth0 198.148.81.136): S set, 40 headers + 0 data bytes
len=44 ip=198.148.81.136 ttl=53 DF id=43320 tos=0 iplen=44
sport=80 flags=SA seq=0 win=65535 rtt=163.0 ms
seq=4116557452 ack=513609534 sum=32e9 urp=0

len=44 ip=198.148.81.136 ttl=50 DF id=44497 tos=0 iplen=44
sport=80 flags=SA seq=1 win=65535 rtt=162.9 ms
seq=3555362188 ack=2032411494 sum=f5c4 urp=0

DUP! len=42 ip=198.148.81.136 ttl=50 id=45735 tos=10 iplen=40
sport=80 flags=A seq=1 win=0 rtt=890.9 ms
seq=4294967295 ack=2032411494 sum=2b36 urp=0
```

Figure 3.3

`#hping3 -c 1 -V -p 80 -s 5050 -A VICTIM_IP`

-- this type of scan sends a single TCP packet of type ACK (-A) and helps us figure out if a device is up on the network when it does not respond to ping (it is blocked by a firewall).

The arguments of the command (Figure 3.4) represent:

- **-c 1**: sends only one packet
- **-V**: verbose
- **-p 80**: sets the destination port to 80 (HTTP)
- **-s 5050**: sets the source port to 5050
- **-A**: sends TCP ACK packets

```
root@rn-s-1vcpu-1gb-fra1-01:~# hping3 -c 10 -V -p 80 -s 5050 -A hackthisite.com
using eth0, addr: 46.101.143.160, MTU: 1500
HPING hackthisite.com (eth0 52.86.22.136): A set, 40 headers + 0 data bytes
len=42 ip=52.86.22.136 ttl=236 DF id=49647 tos=0 iplen=40
sport=80 flags=R seq=0 win=0 rtt=106.6 ms
seq=1866469472 ack=0 sum=5313 urp=0

len=42 ip=52.86.22.136 ttl=239 DF id=49717 tos=0 iplen=40
sport=80 flags=R seq=1 win=0 rtt=105.5 ms
seq=1569963852 ack=0 sum=1276 urp=0

len=42 ip=52.86.22.136 ttl=239 DF id=49943 tos=0 iplen=40
sport=80 flags=R seq=2 win=0 rtt=105.4 ms
seq=166285298 ack=0 sum=1639 urp=0

^C
--- hackthisite.com hping statistic ---
3 packets transmitted, 3 packets received, 0% packet loss
round-trip min/avg/max = 105.4/105.8/106.6 ms
root@rn-s-1vcpu-1gb-fra1-01:~#
```

Figure 3.4

If we want to **cover our traces** (to be anonymous, not to know where the scanning / attack comes from) we can add the **--rand-source** argument:

#hping3 **-c** **1** **-V** **-p** **80** **-s** **5050** **-A** **--rand-source**
VICTIM_IP

Hping3 gives you the opportunity to be very specific with what you do. For example, if we use TCP-like scans at the server level, then we can use TCP messages (such as SYN, ACK, FIN, RST, URG, etc.).

I repeat what I said at the beginning of this book: *IT IS VERY IMPORTANT UNDERSTAND HOW TECHNOLOGY WORKS*. In this case, I refer specifically to the OSI model, the TCP protocol, the ports, etc.

But with **packages sent customized** (an unexpected TCP ACK for example), we can capture the firewall or the application (e.g., the web server) and give us a response with which we can find more information about it (a server on Windows responds in - a different way than one on Linux etc. - example of remote OS fingerprinting).

Next, I suggest you play with these Nmap and hping3 programs to do a little more research so you can understand their usefulness and how they work.

With **hping3** we can also do **DoS** attacks (which we talked about in chapter 5), in which we are flooding a particular device:

```
# hping3 -V -c 2000000 -d 100 -S -w 64 -p 443 -s 591 --flood --rand-source VICTIM_IP
```

And the arguments of this command are:

- --flood: sends the packets as fast as possible
- --rand-source: generates a random source IP address for each packet
- -V: offers more information
- -c --count: the total number of packets
- -d --data: the size of the packets
- -S --syn: TCP SYN packets
- -w --win: window size (default 64)
- -p --destport: destination port
- -s --baseport: source port (by default it's a random one)

These were just a few examples. Now you can start playing with this tool (I recommend using Kali Linux and starting with your local network). Instead of IP_VICTIMA you can give your Router IP or a phone / laptop / server from your network.

PS: if you use Linux (and not Kali Linux) you can install Nmap or hping3 using the command:

```
#sudo apt-get install nmap hping3
```

Why do we want to scan the network ?

Because we can use this information to decide our focus when it comes to penetration testing. What do we focus on? What is the most vulnerable target in the network and what apps there are on it that we can take advantage of? For a hacker (whether ethical or not), the answer to these questions is extremely important.

Why? Because if he is not well informed about the network and the components in it, Hacker will lose its time with certain parts that cannot be exploited and risk being detected. This scanning process is part of the Penetration Testing cycle, which consists of 5 steps (Figure 3.5).

Figure 3.5

IV. Malware and Cyber Attacks

In this chapter, we start talking about **malware types**, and later on we will discuss **Cyber Attacks**. For starters, we will discuss Viruses, Trojans, Worms, Ransomware and other types of programs that were badly designed. But first of all, let us answer the following question:

1) What is a Malware ?

A **malware** (aka. malicious software) is a malicious software program designed to steal, destroy, or corrupt data stored on our devices.

Figure 4.1

Many people use the **generic term of the virus,** which is not necessarily correct because there can be many types of dangerous programs. Here below (only) a part of them:

1) *Virus*
2) *Trojans*
3) *Worms*
4) *Ransomware*
5) *Spyware*
6) *Adware*
7) *and many more (Rootkit, time bombs, backdoor, etc.)*

Here is the picture below on *Wikipedia*, the proportion (in 2011) of malware from the Internet. Since then, many things have changed or changed, but it's interesting to have such a hierarchy with the most common types of malware.

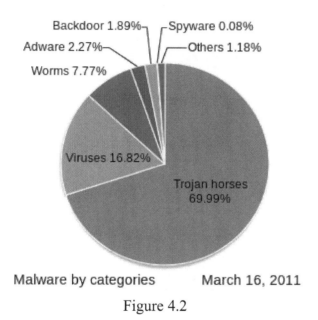

Malware by categories   March 16, 2011

Figure 4.2

And now take some of these malware and discuss them in more detail:

1) Viruses

A virus is a program with which we are all accustomed to. Whether we had the computer infected with a virus or that we heard / seen someone else, we know that these viruses can be really dangerous for us (and especially for our data stored on the computer - the most important element for us).

Virus programmers take advantage of existing vulnerabilities in different operating systems (especially Windows) and write software to take advantage of them (and users of these devices).

2) Trojans

A Trojan is a type of program designed to appear for the benefit of the person who uses it, but there is a malicious code behind that has other intentions altogether. These types of programs are most common in the Internet (as you could see in the picture above) and are used to being easily masked in front of an inexperienced user. So in the (first) run of the program, the trojan is installed and will hide, doing its job "quietly". The term Trojan comes from the story of the Trojan horse in Greek mythology, exposed in the movie Troy.

3) Worms

A worm is a form of malware that once it infects a device (PC, laptop, server, etc.) will do its best to expand and infect others on the network. Thus, a worm manages to **slow networks** and the connected devices (by using CPU and RAM resources) and even the network, because infected computers will generate abnormal traffic.

4) Ransomware

A more popular type of malware lately is ransomware, whose purpose is to **encrypt the hard disk** (or SSD) victims and to request a cash **redeem** for the decryption key.

5) Adware

There are programs that once installed on a device (or in the browser) will start to show commercials (annoying).

6) Spyware

Spyware are programs designed to extract certain data from users. They are not meant to hurt (by consuming resources) or affect the victim in any way, but simply extract data and send them to "mother servers" (those who have initiated "espionage").

First, you need to be aware of the existence of such programs, after which you have to take protection / prevention measures against them.

In this situation, anti-virus programs are very welcome because they contain very large databases (called signatures) that check every program / file on your operating system (Windows, Linux or Mac).

Now you can also know that Windows has the highest number of malware (viruses, Trojans, ransomware, etc.). Why? Because Windows is the most widely used operating system in the world, and hackers have something to "steal." That's why the main focus of attackers and cyber-security companies is on Windows.

The Mac and Linux are also not free from malware, but their number is not that big. They have been designed with a higher degree of security in mind and operate completely differently from Windows.

2) Examples of Cyber Attacks

In this section of Chapter 4, we'll talk about Cyber Attacks and we'll see some examples of **Cyber Attacks** (and hacking methods) from the Internet. These hacking methods are very common, and each one serves a particular purpose.

What is a Cyber Attack?

A cyber attack is a means by which a person (with evil intentions) takes advantage of the **vulnerabilities** existing on a particular system (server, computer, network equipment, application, etc.)

Here are some of the most common attacks on the Internet:
1)**MITM-M**an **in t**he Middle
2)**DoS-D**enial **of S**ervice
3)**DDoS-D**istributed **D**enial **of S**ervice,check this link: http://www.digitalattackmap.com/
4)**SQLi-**SQL injection
5)**XSS-**Cross-Site Scripting

In addition, there are many more in the Internet world, but to illustrate some, we will only focus on the top 3. So let's take the first type of attack, MITM, and discuss it in more detail about it (and show you some ways you can make such attacks - but please do it in an ethical way), after which will go further with the discussion and discuss DoS and DDoS.

What is a MITM (Man In The Middle) attack ?

MITM is a type of cyber attack in order to listen to the traffic of users connected to the same network.

What this means? It means that if you go to a café in town, someone can connect with you to the same Wi-Fi, and from just a few commands you can see all your conversations on Facebook, Google, etc.

That's how it is, but do not worry because things are not that simple. Why? Because the vast majority of our Internet connections are secured (**HTTPS instead of HTTP**;)), instead it does not mean that there can be no one listening to your traffic.

To avoid such situations, I recommend that you use a VPN in public places. In Figure 4.3 you can see an example of an MITM attack:

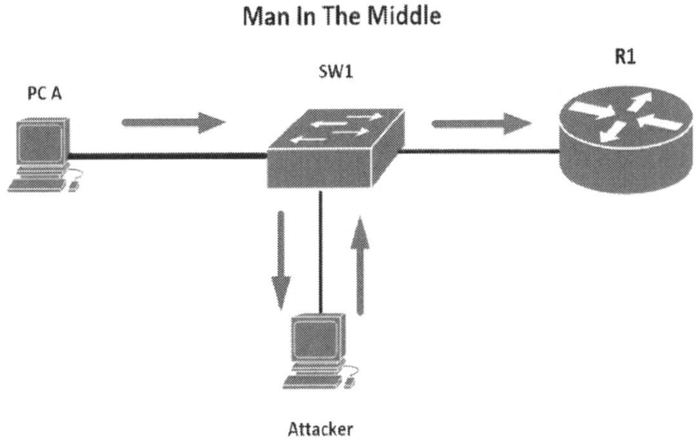

Man In The Middle

Figure 4.3

There are several ways you can do MITM (I will list below just a few of the many possibilities below):

- **MAC Spoofing**
- **ARP Spoofing**
- **Rogue DHCP Server**
- **STP Attack**
- **DNS Poisoning**

These are some of the most common. In the following I will discuss some of these and I will give you some practical examples of how to do it.

1) MAC Spoofing

The term spoofing comes from deceiving, and in this case it refers to the deception of at least one device in the network by the fact that a certain computer is given as another computer (or even Router) using its MAC address.

This can be done very easily using a program that changes your MAC address with a PC to see its traffic. Here's an example (https://windowsreport.com/mac-address-changer-windows-10/) on Windows 10 about how to change your MAC address, but in my opinion the process is much more complex, compared to Linux:

```
# ifconfig eth0 down
# macchanger -m 00:d0:70:00:20:69 eth0
# ifconfig eth0 up
```

First,we stop the interface (eth0 in this example), then we use the **macchanger** command that helps us with the **MAC address change**, and the -m argument lets us specify an address. For verification, use the command: **#ifconfig**

PS: If you want to **generate a random MAC**, then use: **#macchanger -r eth0**

2) ARP Spoofing

ARP Spoofing works in a similar way to MAC spoofing, just as the attacker uses the ARP protocol to mislead the entire network about having the MAC address X (which is actually the Router). Thus, all network devices that want to reach the Internet will send the traffic to the attacker (which will redirect it to Router). In this situation, the attacker can see all the traffic passing through him using a traffic capture program such as Wireshark.

In Figure 4.4 below, you can see how this process takes place:

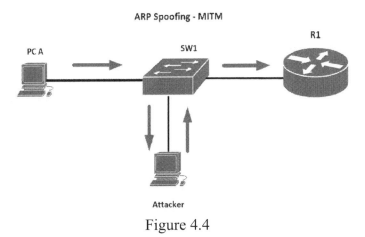

Figure 4.4

To initiate such an attack first we must **start the routing process on Linux** so that traffic can be sent from the victim to the Router and vice versa (through us, the "attackers"):

```
# echo "1" > /proc/sys/net/ipv4/ip_forward
# cat /proc/sys/net/ipv4/ip_forward
```

Now we are **redirecting** the traffic to the port we want to listen to:

```
# iptables -t nat -A PREROUTING -p tcp --destination-port 80 -j REDIRECT --to-port 8181
```

After which we need to install the program:

```
# sudo apt-get update
```

```
# sudo apt-get install dsniff
```

And now we can give the command to start the attack:

```
# sudo arpspoof -i etho -t 192.168.1.3 192.168.1.1
```

```
# sudo arpspoof -i etho -t 192.168.1.1 192.168.1.3
```

- *-i eth0*: is the interface on which we will start the attack

- *-t 192.168.1.3*: is the IP of the victim (the device we want to attack - CHANGE with an IP from your network)
- *192.168.1.1*: is the Router IP (CHANGE the Router IP to your Router)

Virtually these two orders, send fake packages to the two devices informing them that traffic has to pass through the attacker. Now all you have to do is open Wireshark and see how the victim's traffic "passes through you".

Here is another need for an element that will facilitate the **DECRYPTION of traffic**. Why? Because much of the Internet traffic is encrypted.

With this tool we will use: **SSLstrip** (removes the security element, SSL), and the command to decrypt HTTPS traffic in HTTP is:

sudo python **sslstrip.py -l 8181**

This command will listen to traffic on port 8181 and try to decrypt it. After that, you can start Wireshark and see the encrypted traffic (however, I suggest you start Wireshark and when the traffic is encrypted to see the difference).

PS: With a simple search on Google you will find SSLstrip;)

To write the result to a file (from the terminal) you can use a tool similar to Wireshark called **Ettercap**. Once you install it on Linux you can give the following command:

sudo **ettercap –i eth0 –T -w /root/scan.txt –M arp /192.168.1.3 /**

The arguments used in the command are:

- *-i eth0*: the interface on which traffic is listened
- -T : to launch command execution over the terminal
- -M : Man in middle mode
- -w : writing data to a file
- 192.168.1.3: the victim's IP address

3) Rogue DHCP Server

This type of attack involves creating an unauthorized DHCP Server in the network that offers the valid IP address, but which offers the IP address of the gateway, the address of the attacker. Thus, each network device (which has requested an IP address dynamically) will send the traffic to the attacker, which will then redirect to the Router. Meanwhile, all traffic can be **decrypted** (using SSL Strip) and seen using **Wireshark**.

This attack can be done by using (on Windows) a program that allows you to create the DHCP server, and on Linux you can use the **dhcpd server**. Besides all this, you also need to add a static default route to **redirect** all traffic to the Network Router (aka Gateway).

Here are the steps:
1. Start the Routing process on Kali
   a. # echo "1" > /proc/sys/net/ipv4/ip_forward
2. Install the DHCP server
   a. # sudo **apt-get install isc-dhcp-server**
3. Configure the DHCP server
   a. # nano /etc/dhcp/dhcpd.conf
4. Add a (default) static route to your Router
   a. # sudo **ip route add default via** 192.168.1.1
5. Start SSL Strip
6. Capture the traffic

How can we protect ourselves from a MITM attack?

Yes, there is a solution for all these attacks. In fact, several solutions, but I will tell you a relatively simple one that you can use from today. It's called VPN (Virtual Private Network) and it will encrypt your traffic without anyone (in the middle) being able to decrypt it.

Another solution applies to Network switches, namely DHCP Snooping or DAI (Dynamic ARP Inspection), which are different mechanisms to rely on certain devices in the network. And if someone wants to break this, then they will be penalized by excluding them completely from the network (closing the port directly from the switch).

What is a DoS (Denial of Service) attack?

DoS is a form of cyber attack with the purpose of **interrupting** (for an amount of time) the operation of a particular service on a server, with only **one source of traffic** (the attack is done on a single computer). The DoS takes place by **sending** an **impressive** amount of **traffic** to a targeted service in order to interrupt it. Thus, receiving a lot of requests, a web server for example,would not handle and block at the moment => interruption of the service (in this case dropping the website). Here's an example of attack in Figure 4.5:

DoS

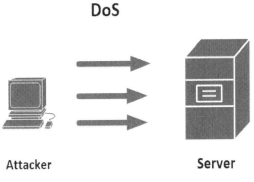

Attacker · · · · · Server

Figure 4.5

What is a DDoS (Distributed Denial of Service) attack?

DDoS is a form of cyber attack to interrupt (for a period of time) the operation of a particular service on a server or on an entire network, with many Internet traffic sources. DDoS takes place via multiple "infected" computers with malware that send an impressive number of Gbps (10.40, 100+ Gbps - greatly depends on the number of computers) in traffic.

These computers are all over the world and do not have a specific location, which is one of the reasons why DDoS is very hard to fight. Even recently (in February 2018), the biggest DDoS attack in history, cataloging 1.5 Tbps (or 1500 Gbps), has taken place. Wow!

Coming back, I want you to know that such a network of malware-infected computers are called Botnet. Below is an example of a Botnet that can serve multiple malicious purposes (sending spam or malware or a significant Gbps number for DoS) - Figure 4.6:

DDoS

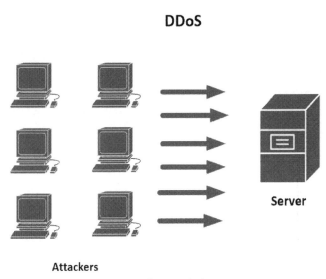

Figure 4.6

In addition to these network-related attacks, there are also attacks to "break" passwords:

1) **Brute Force**
2) **Dictionary Attack**
3) **Rainbow table**

1) Brute Force

Brute Force is a form of cyber attack that aims to gain unauthorized access to the system (a site administration server, server, network equipment, etc.). This technique uses "brute force," meaning the attacker tries to **guess** the **password** with a minimum of logic behind. Often, this technique leads to failure and waiver by the attacker, but there are many cases where access to the system is prevented because it has not changed its default password (which is often "admin" or "12345678")

2) Dictionary attack

A Dictionary Attack goes a little bit more targeted on the victim's system because there are several external factors that relate to that organization / person.

With the help of some tools, hundreds or even thousands of words can be generated that can be tried to get access to the system. The **disadvantage** of this type of attack is that it can take a long time (depending on the number of words and the security of the system), and the dictionary does not guarantee the success of the attack.

An easy way to **combat** these types of attacks is to use a maximum number (usually 3) of login attempts in the system.

3) Rainbow table

The third type of attack is called "**Rainbow Table**" which aims to "**decipher**" a **hash**. Do you still know what a hash is? If not, I'll briefly summarize.

A hash is a unique value of a word (or any combination of letters / digits, etc.). Any combination of letters, numbers, words / phrases in this world will generate a unique value. Well, now think about your password when you enter it into your Facebook, Google, etc. account.

All companies do not store your password directly into their database (because it involves a security risk) but they will store this hash (of the password). When an attacker "steals" the database, he steals it with **username** and *password* *hash* (and not the password in clear text).

Thus the attacker will use a hash list to decipher the hash-passwords from the stolen database. This list is called "rainbow table" and tries to find out which is the password.

And now you may be wondering, "Why are things so?" The answer is simple: because the hash process is irreversible, that is, once the hash has been generated, we cannot enter it using the same mathematical formula and get the password.

So the attacker tries his luck with his list of hashes (rainbow tables) that are associated with passwords.
In the next chapter, we'll move on to the first step toward generating a cyber attack, and we'll talk about Scanning. Also, towards the end of the chapter I will show you how to do a DoS pin attack using (Kali) Linux.

Or <u>Click Here to Download</u>

Also, I kindly ask you to **leave a review** after finishing this book. It will help me a lot. Thank you and happy reading ! ☺

Enjoyed the book? Please leave a Review on Amazon.com

If you received value from this book, tshen I'd like to ask you for a favour. Would you be kind enough to leave a review for this book on Amazon.

Click here here to leave a Review on Amazon.com
(https://amzn.to/2H9NOWX)

I would like to thank you for reading this book and reaching to the end of it (trust me when I say, that not many people manage to get this far away).

Also, I want to reach as many people as I can with this book (my goal is 10.000 people in the next 3 years). That's a lot of people and without you and your review I won't be able to achieve that.

Not only that, but you will receive some good karma that sooner or later will manifest into your life.

Thank you! Ramon Nastase

Made in the USA
Lexington, KY
13 September 2019